Poison Dart Frogs

A Guide to Care and Breeding

Jason Juchems

**Herpetological
Publishing**

Poison Dart Frogs: A Guide to Care and Breeding
Copyright © 2011 by Jason Juchems. All rights reserved.

Cover Design: Copyright © 2011 by Jason Juchems
Image Design: Copyright © 2011 by Jason Juchems
Photography Copyright © 2011 by Jason Juchems
Book Design: Copyright © 2011 by Jason Juchems

ISBN: 978-0-615-42217-6
LCCN: 2010919226

First Edition January 2011, (revised).

Printed in the United States of America

Herpetological Publishing
PO Box 1507
Pekin, IL 61555

Table of Contents

Acknowledgment

I would like to start my book by thanking those who have inspired me into the hobby of herpetoculture and the science of herpetology.

To my grandfather Roland Juchems, without you I would not have chased snakes, had my first pet turtle, and hiked through the woods in search or reptiles and amphibians. You let me learn through nature and taught me what it is to love nature.

To my wife for her support and patience, thank you. The basement speaks for itself, and thanks for putting up with it.

To my family for putting up with me and the collection, my parents who had hundreds of animals snuck into the house and the occasional frog that got loose. That is all I will admit that was lost in the house.

Justin Reeise and Justin Smith, thanks for your contributions, conversations, and constant experimentations with husbandry. Over years of working with dart frogs, geckos, and other herps we have spent plenty of time bouncing ideas.

To my friends who have to listened to my useless facts and rants.

Introduction

By far, one of the most recognized animals of the tropical rain forest is the poison dart frog. These tiny jewels live in remote areas of the tropical rain forest. Through leaf litter, bromeliads, and streams, these little wonders of the world make their homes in one of the most beautiful areas on earth. In their habitat, they are surrounded by tall trees that form a canopy. Many organisms of the rain forest have adapted to live in trees. The rain forest holds more biodiversity than any other ecosystem. Diverse organisms thrive in the rain forest environment because steady temperatures and large amounts of rainfall create an ideal climate, especially for cold blooded creatures. Days in the tropical rain forest are filled with warmth and rain showers, with temperatures that drop slightly during the night. Daily showers and average temperatures of around 77°F (25°C) result in a humid environment. The yearly rainfall can range from 6 to 30 feet (1.8-9.1 m). Understanding the dynamics of this important ecosystem allows captive care and breeding of poison dart frogs to become quite simple.

Ranitomeya imitator in a bromeliad.

Chapter 1: About Poison Dart Frogs

Poison dart frogs belong to a class of animals known as amphibians. Amphibians are a fascinating group of animals that drink water through their skin. Tiny pores in amphibians' skin allow them to accomplish this unique task. The pores also allow amphibians to keep themselves moist by not only retaining water on their skin, but by secreting water through their skin too. This is a vital part of an amphibian's life. It is important that a person does not pick up and handle a wild amphibian. The salts and oils of human skin can be lethal to these animals. In addition, minimal amounts of soaps and detergents are lethal to amphibians because their skin is very delicate. When keeping amphibians, handling should be kept to a minimum.

Poison dart frogs, also called poison arrow frogs, get their name from the poisonous toxins they secrete through their skin. The natives of Colombia, the Embera or 'Choco,' use these frogs by rubbing blowgun darts across the frogs' skin to gain toxins to hunt for monkeys, iguanas, and other food. It seems the practice of tipping arrows with frog toxins is isolated to Colombia. Only three species of poison dart frogs are used for tipping darts. These beautiful frogs use their small tongues to eat ants, termites, beetles, aphids, and any other tiny insects they may be able to find. The frogs gain their toxins from the insects, primarily ants, which they eat in the wild. Ants are high in formic acid. It is believed that part of the poison is derived from plants the ants eat. Once they are brought into captivity, in zoos and homes, dart frogs lose their toxic abilities as their diet changes.

Dart frogs can be found throughout rain forests spanning from Costa Rica to Brazil and Peru to Panama. These tiny creatures range in color from bright reds and blues to duller grays and blacks. Frogs of the same species may have different colorations depending on their habitat. Groups of frogs that live in isolated locations, or pockets, vary in color and are referred to as morphs. In the hobby of keeping reptiles and amphibians, morphs are often man-made creations through selective breeding. However, this is not the case for poison dart frogs. Morph labels are names that designate the coloration and native location of a specific frog. The strawberry dart frog, *Oophaga pumilio,* is red with black spots, while the "Blue Jean" morph of the species is red with blue legs. "Blue Jeans," as a color morph, are a small species of dart frog from Costa Rica. These beautiful colors serve a purpose. The colors warn predators of their poisonous nature. Only a few species of large spiders, birds, and the snake species *Leimadophis epinephelus,* can eat these frogs without being affected by their poison.

Adelphobates castaneoticus

In addition to their brilliant color, poison dart frogs can range in size from .25-2 inches (2–50 mm) in adult length. That is to say they can be small enough to fit on a dime, or may be as large as a half dollar. These frogs create a variety of sounds. Some call in high pitch squeaks while the call of other dart frogs is as beautiful as a canary. Over 285 different species of dart frogs can be found. A person cannot be poisoned from simply touching these little jewels because the poison must be ingested or somehow enter the blood stream. However, for the safety of both frog and human it is suggested that humans refrain from touching poison dart frogs.

Commonly Available Species

In the hobby today, there are species that have been established in captivity for 10 to 20 years. Due to recent imports, some morphs have recently become available for the first time, and others for the first time in several years. Recently, the nomenclature has changed for several of these frogs. This section reflects these nomenclature changes and includes a brief overview of the commonly available species in the hobby.

New species have become available through captive breeding projects in their native habitat. Species such as (Left) *Hyloxalus azureiventris* and (Right) *Ameerega pepperi* have been imported from Peru and are now produced in the United States by hobbyists and professional breeders.

(Left) "Green and Bronze" *Dendrobates auratus* (Right) "Black" *Dendrobates auratus* are both newer morphs imported from Panama.

Dendrobates auratus: *Dendrobates auratus* hails from the countries of Panama, Costa Rica, and Nicaragua. In the 1932, *auratus* were introduced to Hawaii. They are established and propagated enough to warrant their own morph. The overwhelming majority of *auratus* frogs available on the market today are descendents from Panama, including the introduced *auratus* in Hawaii. They range in size from 1-1.75 inches (25-45 mm). *Auratus* do well living in groups, but vigilance is needed to ensure no frog is bullied. In the past few years importation from Panama has brought several new color morphs to the hobby. It is no longer just the standard green and black auratus. Now there are various color morphs including a mixture of Blue and Black, Green and Bronze, Spotted, also known as Ancon Hill, Campana, Kahlua & Creme, and a solid Black form of *Dendrobates auratus*. Caution needs to be taken when purchasing these frogs. Several importations have led to a large influx of wild caught animals available to hobbyists at a reasonable price. For those who are new to the hobby, sticking with a captive bred specimen is advised. This reduces the risk of having to treat the frog for parasitic and bacterial infections and ensures a healthy terrarium. Though shy, *Dendrobates auratus* is an excellent beginner frog because of their reasonable pricing and availability for purchase.

The above *Dendrobates tinctorius* show the wide range in natural color morphs.
(Left) "Azereus" (Middle) "Citronella" (Right) "Infer-Alanis"

Dendrobates tinctorius: This species of dart frog covers a variety of different color morphs and even sizes. These frogs typically have a black background with blue legs that are laced with blue or powder blue, and stripes or additional coloration ranging from bright yellowish orange to white. Most reach a snout to vent length of 2 -2.25 inches (50-57 mm). Color morphs include Lemon Drop, Brazilian Yellow Head, Powder Blue, Patricia, Citronella, Alanis, and the classic Surinam Cobalt. *Dendrobates azereus*, once classified as its own species, is now classified as *Dendrobates tinctorius*. Currently there are over 20 different color morphs found in this species. *Dendrobates tinctorius* can be found in Guyana, Suriname, French Guiana, and Brazil. *Tinctorius* are more of a terrestrial species, requiring a horizontal terrarium. Due to their large size, a 20 gallon aquarium is the minimum tank size for a male-female pair. *Tinctorius* are a great species for the beginner enthusiast and should be kept in male-female pairs. Having an additional female may create territorial disputes with fatal consequences.

"Powder Blue"

"Cobalt"

Dendrobates leucomelas

***Dendorbates leucomelas*:**
This species, also known as the Bumble Bee Dart Frog or Leuc for short is a black and yellow banded frog and is a great addition to any terrarium. The call of the *leucomelas* sounds similar to a canary's song. These frogs do well in groups. Multiple males seem to be a bit timid around one another, so it is not uncommon for only one male to call. Leucs are known for being bold, so expect to see theses frogs actively moving around the terrarium. The typical leuc has a snout to vent length of 1.25-1.5 inches (30-38 mm). They are native to Venezuela, Columbia, and Brazil.

Genus *Phyllobates*: The genus *Phyllobates* is comprised of five species, three of which are dangerously toxic. The smallest, *lugubris,* only attains a length of 0.75-1 inches (19-25mm). Species *vittatus* and *aurotaenia* can be a bit shy and have a snout to vent length of   1.2 -1.5 inches (30-38mm). The larger two species, *terribilis* and *bicolor*, are bold species. *Terribilis* can be found in a few different color morphs and range in length from 1.75-2.3 inches (44-58 mm). *Bicolor* range in length from 1.5-2 inches (38-51 mm). *Phyllobates* do well living in groups, but a watchful eye is needed to ensure no frog is bullied. Species *terribilis*, *bicolor*, and *aurotaenia* are the frogs used by the Embera to gain toxins for hunting. Even though dart frogs are considered nontoxic in captivity, always air on the side of caution when handling these dart frogs. It is best to use a net, transfer tube, or pre-rinse plastic gloves when handling dart frogs.

Oophaga pumilio,
"Guarmo River" Panama

Oophaga pumilio: *Pumilio* were once classified as *Dendrobates pumilio*. They are often called strawberry poison dart frogs although they come in many colors. These tiny dart frogs can be found in east central Nicaragua, Panama, and the lowland areas of Costa Rica. Their tiny size is no exaggeration as adult *pumilio* can fit on a U.S. dime. In the 1990s, Costa Rica shut down their borders for wildlife exportation. As a result, the color morph "Blue Jean" became almost non-existent in the hobby. However, due to captive cultivation this species is available, but in very limited numbers. Within recent years, new captive importations from Europe and wild caught specimens from Panama have made *pumilio* a very popular choice. However, recent imports from Panama have added an imposter frog to several wholesale price lists. This imposter frog is very similar to the "Blue Jean" morph of Costa Rica. *Pumilio* are part of a group of frogs called obligated egg feeders. Once their tadpoles hatch, females will lay infertile eggs for the tadpoles to eat. The tadpoles must eat these eggs in order to develop correctly. Due to their size and complexity in breeding, *pumilio* are recommended for advanced keepers. *Pumilio* are an arboreal species requiring a vertical terrarium.

Thumbnail species: In the past few years hobbyists have been excited by these tiny and fascinating little dart frogs. Many of these frogs, propagating in bromeliads, are members of the genus *Ranitomeya*, which was once part of the genus *Dendrobates*. *Ranitomeya* species include *imitator, lamasi, ventrimaculatus, reticulta, fantastica,* and *vanzolini* to name only a few. Even within the species listed there are different color morphs. *Ranitomeya* species can be found in the countries of Guyana, Suriname, French Guiana, Brazil, Ecuador, Colombia, Peru, and Panama. Thumbnail species are similar in size to that of *pumilio*. Due to their size, thumbnail species are recommended for intermediate and advanced keepers. Thumbnail species are primarily arboreal so a vertical terrarium is required. Thumbnails and *pumilio* can be kept in groups, but competing females may stomp out each other's eggs. A female frog literally uses her hind legs to kick, push, and destroy the eggs of rival females. Careful observation is needed to ensure no frog is being bullied when kept in groups.

Ranitomeya imitator

Mixing Species

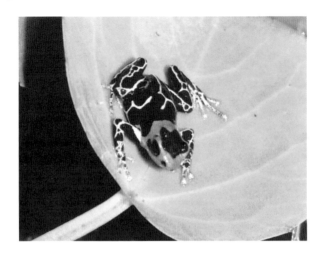

Ranitomeya fantastica

Housing mixed species or color morphs of dart frogs together is not recommended, although it is a topic of much debate among hobbyists. Many people feel they have invested good money in their animals and believe they should be able to house them any way they like. Others feel a greater responsibility to the hobby, rather than the will of the individual hobbyist. The reason for not mixing species is primarily to stop the hybridization of dart frog species and out-crossing morphs. Since each morph represents a geographical location, mixing morphs muddies the water of the origins of dart frogs. Breeding a "Powder Blue" and "Cobalt" together is possible since they are the same species. This creation would be an outcross and is not accepted in the hobby just as hybridization. Within the same species, morphs may represent different sizes of frogs, not just color. Larger frogs may display aggression toward smaller frogs by eating more and bullying them over territory. Care must also be taken not to mix color morphs from different importations. The blue and black *auratus* can be found in several different pockets across the country of Panama. It is advised to find offspring, originating from the same importation to minimize the risk of mixing races from different localities in the same country. Housing mixed species or morphs is acceptable when rearing young froglets, taking care to ensure that morphs similar in appearance are not housed together or accidentally mislabeled, or that any individual frog is being bullied. Many zoos display their dart frogs in mixed species exhibits. These are often large enclosures housing young frogs. Older frogs establish territory and have more size to defend their space. Zoos often utilize a mixed species tank due to the limited amount of space they have to display animals. The specimens on display are also not being introduced to breeding conditions.

Chapter 2: Terrarium Habitat

Setting up the terrarium for a frog is one of the most rewarding, time consuming, and expensive aspects involved in the care of dart frogs. There are several terrarium options available to hobbyists ranging from the traditional aquarium to an open front glass terrarium design favored by many herp keepers. Both of these styles are readily available at a local pet store. The type of terrarium selected usually depends on budget. Each design will require some sort of fruit fly proofing, or soon the frogs will go hungry. The following steps explain how to create a simple terrarium design for a dart frog habitat.

Step 1: The Tank

Begin by acquiring a tank. This build uses a 10 gallon aquarium measuring 20 × 10 × 12 inches. These tanks work great for smaller dart frogs and rearing tanks for larger frogs such as *tincorious*. Once larger frogs reach adult size, a 20 gallon or larger tank is recommended. Commercially available glass terrariums measuring 12×12×18 inches and 18×18×24 inches are used by the author for *O. pumilio* and thumbnail species. Aquarium tanks can be purchased at a local pet store. Make sure to clean out the inside of the tank using a mixture of 1 cup bleach to 1 gallon of water and a clean sponge or rag. Even a new aquarium, that appears clean, should be cleaned out before it is used for an animal habitat.

Step 2: Drainage Layer (using LECA or aquarium gravel)

A drainage layer needs to be added to the tank to hold excess water left over from misting. LECA (Lightweight Expanded Clay Agregate), a product designed for hydroponic gardening, can be used to create this layer. These aggregate clay balls are a great solution for creating a drainage layer because they are so lightweight. This product needs to be rinsed before use. Pictured is a mixture of washed and unwashed LECA. The dull red LECA was not washed, while the bright red clay balls were washed. The LECA should be 1.5-2 inches deep. For a 10 gallon tank, about 2 full gallon sized freezer bags of LECA are required. Bulk LECA can be purchased in 50 liter bags and a smaller gray colored product is making its way into pet shops. If LECA cannot be obtained, then aquarium gravel can be substituted instead. Before adding a drainage layer, a bulkhead fitting hole may need to be added as an outlet for the extra water that collects at the bottom of the tank. This requires drilling glass and should be completed by a person who has experience doing such work. Tanks above 10 gallons use tempered glass and require special equipment. If a bulkhead fitting is not used then a siphon can be used instead to drain excess water when it accumulates. If a siphon will be used, then installing a PVC canal can be helpful. In one corner of the tank vertically place a section of ½ inch PVC pipe measuring approximately 3-4 inches tall. The PVC pipe can be used as a tube to gain

access to the bottom of the tank when siphoning water. A cap should be attached to the top of the PVC channel to prevent debris from collecting in the tube between siphoning. When using a siphon, be sure the siphon is only used for this tank and the drainage pail and siphon is sanitized after each use with a solution of 1 cup bleach to 1 gallon water.

Step 3: Substrate Barrier

A variety of different ideas for substrate barriers can be found online and in other texts. In the author's experience, landscaping fabric is the best material to use to create a substrate barrier. This product is offered seasonally at local hardware and chain stores. When purchasing landscaping fabric, choose a fabric with a minimal three year guarantee. Simply cut the fabric to the desired size and place it on top of the drainage layer. Apply a double to triple of fabric. In addition, cut enough fabric to add a bit of a lip to all four sides of the tank. Instead of landscaping fabric, fiberglass screen can also be used. However, do not use aluminum screen as it is not safe for this application.

Step 4: Substrate/Media

For groundcover, use a mixture of fir and sphagnum peat moss mix and coco fiber. These products can be purchased at a pet shop. Premix the substrate in a pail using two parts fir and sphagnum to one part coco fiber. If a premade mixture of fir and sphagnum cannot be found, a homemade version can be created by using a blender to blend reptile fir tree bark, or orchid bark, with sphagnum peat moss purchased in a garden center in equal parts. Once mixed, add the substrate to the center of the tank on top of the landscaping fabric. This reduces the amount of substrate that may slip down the sides of the tank. A depth of 1-1.5 inch of substrate is typical. For plants with larger roots, 2 inches of substrate, or more, may be required. Finish by spreading the media evenly. If a bulkhead fitting is not used, then keep one edge of fabric uncovered to use as a "pull tab" to lift the landscaping fabric up to siphon out excess water when the drainage layer becomes full. To create hills for live moss or other plants move substrate to the desired height. After the media has been arranged, heavily mist the tank.

Step 5: Plants, Furnishings, and Microfauna

After the desired level of substrate has been added to the tank, it is time to begin planting. Include plants to provide hiding places for frogs and add color to the tank. Keep in mind, plants grow! Do not overplant the tank. As a rule of thumb for a first tank, include plants that require low light and are easy to grow. Also, consider the type of lighting fixture that will be used. The lighting should be designed to stimulate plant growth and to add a little heat. Commercially available florescent aquarium hoods and terrarium fixtures work well. Fixtures designed for compact florescent coiled bulbs are also safe to use. Twenty-six watt bulbs seem to work best, but check the fixture's wattage maximum before bulb installation. For those with larger collections, 48 inch shop lights are a good alternative to traditional aquarium hoods because they can efficiently light more than one tank. Florescent 5000 – 6500K tube daylight bulbs are needed for a shop light. UV bulbs are not a necessity for lighting fixtures because UV lighting cannot pass through glass. Furnishings such as climbing branches, a rock water bowl, and a coconut hut with petri dish should be added at this time. Also consider whether microfauna will be introduced to the tank. Microfauna are a hot topic among hobbyists today. Two types that are used are isopods and springtails. They work as cleaners in the tank and as an alternate food source. They can be added during step 4 or 5 of the tank set up. If microfauna are added, it is best to let the tank set for 3-4 weeks. This allows time to establish a culture of microfauna within the tank before adding frogs.

Step 6: Fruit Fly Proof Lid

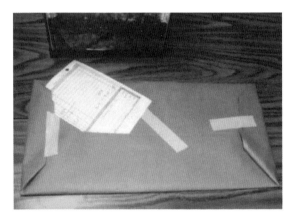

The lid of the tank must fit perfectly to prevent fruit flies from escaping. Use a piece of glass to create the lid. Custom cut glass can be purchased from a local glass shop or hardware store. The cost is reasonable and cheaper than modifying an aquarium glass canopy. Aqueon® (All-Glass®) and Perfecto® aquariums are the most common tanks on the market. Each company has its own dimensions. Be sure to make accurate measurements before ordering cut glass. The glass will be very sharp unless polished. Having the edges of the glass polished by stone is a good safety measure to prevent both the keeper and frogs from getting cut by rough edges. Add a handle to the glass that will allow the lid to be easily lifted. A plastic handle with an adhesive strip can be purchased from a local pet shop or online. Make sure the lid fits properly before adding frogs to the tank.

Step 7: Add Frogs

Before introducing frogs to the tank, heavily mist everything. Next, carefully place frogs in their new enclosure. As a general rule of thumb one adult frog for every 10 gallons of aquarium size. However, many people recommend a 20 gallon tank for a pair of frogs. This recommendation can vary by species. For example, an 18×18×24 inch terrarium can be used for a pair of *pumilio*, while a pair of thumbnails can be housed in a 10 gallon vertical tank or a 12×12×18 inch terrarium. After frogs have been added to the tank, secure the lid and set the lighting fixture on top. Enjoy the product of all the hard work that went into creating the tank! Given time, a hobbyist may be lucky enough to watch breeding behavior, hear calling, and even find eggs. Other terrarium designs can be used along with backgrounds. Instructions for these techniques can be found in the "Additional Notes" section.

Maintenance

When designing a terrarium for poison dart frogs, there are many aspects to keep in mind in terms of maintenance such as water quality, humidity levels, temperature, light cycles, and routine cleaning. Water quality is one of the most important aspects in the husbandry of any amphibian. Different hobbyists use different techniques for providing water and misting for their frogs. Begin by ensuring the water used for dart frogs is amphibian safe. This can be achieved by leaving water out for several days, or using a chemical de-chlorinate that can be purchased at a local pet store. Others use reverse osmosis or natural spring water purchased from a local grocery or bottled water service. Those who use reverse osmosis water may elect to use a product like R/O Right to add minerals back into reverse osmosis water. Do not use distilled water as it may cause bloating issues that may have fatal consequences. For those with large collections, a misting system similar to those in the produce section of the grocery store may be utilized. Reasonably priced misting systems have made it to the market for those with smaller collections. Prices normally start at around $100 for such a system that can handle 2-3 tanks. When using a misting system a hole for the nozzle must be made in the lid. In addition, a siphon line or bulkhead must be installed to drain excess water from the drainage layer. For those with a small collection, a simple spray bottle or yard sprayer may be used to mist the tank once or twice a day.

As a tropical species, dart frogs enjoy relatively high humidity. This can be accomplished by daily misting, using an under tank heater, using a fogger, or a mixture of these techniques. Keeping a small amount of water in the drainage layer also helps keep the humidity high. Foggers and under tank heaters are available from several reptile product companies. Under tank heaters should be placed beneath the tank, however do not directly attach the heater to the glass because this can cause the glass to shatter. Humidity should stay above 80%. Humidity and temperature should be monitored by purchasing a simple hydrometer/thermometer combo gauge and placing the probe in the terrarium. Temperatures should range between 74-84°F (23-29°C) during the day and 68-72°F (20-23°C) during the night. A day-night cycle of 12 hours light and 12 hours night can be achieved by using a household timer purchased from a hardware store. Changes can be made to the day/night cycle to simulate the changes of the season. However, dart frogs are from the equatorial region where the day/night cycle only changes a few hours and the seasons consists of a lengthy rainy and short dry season. This season cycle plays a role in the breeding habits of poison dart frogs.

Simple, ongoing care of the terrarium will be needed over time. Feces on leaves of live plants can be sprayed off with a hand sprayer or wiped off with a clean paper towel. As the water level increases in the drainage layer water will need to be drained through the bulkhead or siphoned. Plants will grow and need to be trimmed or replaced. Algae growth tends to be an issue in all set-ups as growth builds up on the glass and on plants. Using white vinegar or lemon juice on a paper towel to wipe down the side of the glass and plants will help stop algae growth and clean-up the growing infestation. Mist heavily afterwards to remove any heavy build-up. Whenever completing maintenance, frogs should be removed for their protection.

Chapter 3: Feeding

Food and nutrition are extremely important to the development and health of dart frogs. Proper nutrition will allow the hobbyist to enjoy frogs for years to come, and even aid in the prospect of future offspring. Dart frogs have a small, narrow tongue, so small insects are required for feeding. Fruit flies are a staple of the dart frog diet. Other insects are also available to feed dart frogs, some that were not available just a few years ago such as bean weevils. Providing variety in diet is important for the development of healthy frogs. Dart frogs need to be fed daily to every other day. Always have food available and have a source in place for an emergency food supply. The following feeder insects can be purchased through mail order and online.

Fruit Flies: Fruit flies are an essential component of a dart frog's diet. They can be purchased and then cultured at home. A search online can produce several different techniques for culturing fruit flies, along with a list of suppliers. In the "Additional Notes" section, a simple fruit fly media recipe and guide to creating insect culturing cups, that the author uses and has modified over the years, is provided. Small vials of fruit flies can be purchased at some pet stores, but are expensive and do not contain enough flies to maintain a steady diet. When feeding from insect culturing cups or deli cups, gently lift a portion of the lid without removing the lid completely. Hold the open portion of the culture over a deli cup that contains a small amount of vitamin powder and carefully tap about a dime to quarter size amount of flies into the deli cup. Tap the bottom of the culture to knock the remaining flies to the bottom and secure the lid. Gently swirl the open deli cup around until the flies are coated with vitamin powder and then tap these flies into the frog's enclosure. The amount of flies depends on the species and number of frogs in a terrarium. In larger terrariums, typically a dime size portion of flies is needed for every adult frog. Observe the tank to make sure there are extra flies for feeding at later times.

Culturing weevils is simple but they can be difficult to feed off.

Bean Weevils: The bean weevil is an additional source of nutrition that has become recently available for purchase online. Bean weevils are small and easy to reproduce. The best culturing material is dried blacked peas. These can be purchased in the bean section of a local grocer. Rinse peas before use and allow them to dry for 24 hours. Once they have dried, place 1-1½ inches of peas in an insect culturing cup. Next, pour about ¼ inch of peas from an established culture of bean weevils into the cup. Make sure a couple dozen or so weevils are added. In about 4 weeks this will be a producing culture of bean weevils. Please note that bean weevils are considered an agricultural pest and are not legal in all areas. Check state and local laws before acquiring a culture. If the decision is made to discontinue using bean weevils, they need to be disposed of properly to ensure they are not released into the environment. Freezing cultures for no less than 72 hours will ensure all weevils are killed before cultures are disposed of. Feeding weevils to frogs can be a bit tricky. Crumpled coffee filters can be added to the culture. When the weevils need to be fed off, pull out the coffee filter and shake it into the terrarium causing weevils to fall into the tank. A sifter can also be used to separate the weevils in the culture from the peas. Shake some of the contents of the culture into a deli cup with small holes punctured into the bottom so the peas cannot get through the holes, but the weevils can. Hold another standard deli cup under the makeshift sifter so the weevils fall into the second cup and can then be poured into the terrarium.

Culture of springtails in coco fiber bedding.

Springtails: Tropical and temperate springtails are available in the hobby today and can be purchased online. The temperate variety is one of the easiest feeder insects to culture and feed. Coco fiber reptile bedding saturated in water works as a culturing media. Place this mixture in a 24-32 oz disposable food storage container. Place springtails across the top of the media. Feed the springtails a few grains of rice. After a few weeks the container will be full of springtails. Be sure to remove the lid weekly to allow air to exchange and to feed the springtails. Natural charcoal can be used in the same way as coco fiber bedding and can be used as a media for both tropical and temperate springtails. When using charcoal, moisten the briskets using de-chlorinated water and leave ½ inch of water at the bottom of the culture. This method works for both varieties. For tropical springtails, feed and open containers in the same method described for temperate springtails. To feed springtails to dart frogs, place a chunk of charcoal or a spoonful of coco fiber into the frog enclosure. Charcoal method users can hold the culture at an angle so that the briskets to do not fall out. Add more water until the culture is draining water into the terrarium with springtails in the water. Tanks should be seeded with springtails prior to frog introduction by a few weeks. Weekly to every other week reseeding may be needed. New cultures should be made every 3-4 months.

Isopods: Isopods are often called "rolly-pollies", "pillbugs", or "sowbugs."They are great tank cleaners of decaying matter and are an alternative food source. These are of the tropical variety, not the ones in your backyard. Isopods can be cultured in a coco fiber, milled sphagnum mixed substrate kept moist. Food such as egg shells, carrots, apple slice, rice, and fish food can be offered. Leaf liter or brown, non printed cardboard works well for hiding placed and collecting for feeding. Leaves or cardboard can be shaken into the tank to feed frogs. Tanks should be seeded with isopods prior to frog introduction by a few weeks. Weekly to every other week reseeding may be needed. New cultures should be made every 3-4 months.

Subterranean Termites: Termites are an excellent food source for dart frogs. They are great for fattening up thin frogs or replenishing females from the burdens of egg laying. However, feeding too many termites can lead to obesity. Although there are different kinds of termites, subterranean termites require humidity and do not thrive if these conditions are not met, making them the best candidate among termites to use as feeders since they will not survive in most homes, except in the south. Termites can live in a deli cup feeding on corrugated cardboard, but caution needs to be taken when dealing with termites in the home. Nobody wants to cause home damage due to lack of vigilance. Place a brick, or similar sized object, in the center of a plastic storage container with the deli cup containing the termites on top of the brick. Fill the plastic storage container with water to create a moat around the deli cup. Add enough water to cover most of the brick, but not the deli cup, so if termites attempt to escape they will drown in the moat rather than cause an infestation in the home. Field collecting termites can also be done in a pesticide free area, however the recommended way of acquiring termites is through purchasing cultures online, not field collection or personal culturing. To feed termites to frogs, tap a small amount of termites into a petri dish and place the dish inside the terrarium. Watch and make sure the frogs consume all the termites. If frogs do not eat all the termites within a short amount of time, feed them fewer termites next time. Since termites can cause such destruction if they escape it is best not to have an excess of termites in the terrarium.

Crickets: Crickets are a common food staple for reptiles and amphibians. Many pet stores have them readily available by the dozen. However, the sizes available are too large for poison dart frogs. Special ordering through an online cricket seller or pet store is the best opportunity to obtain crickets to feed a dart frog collection. Crickets are typically sold in a variety of sizes in quantities starting around 500 crickets. However, cricket counts are actually determined by weight, not individual crickets. The common size needed for dart frogs is pinhead crickets which, as their name suggests, are very small. Crickets can be "gut loaded" by feeding on a quality diet. Feed crickets a diet of romaine lettuce and other high quality produce. Commercially available cricket diet is also available. Through the food chain, nutrients from the crickets' diet can be passed on to dart frogs. Place paper towel tubes arranged sideways in a 10 gallon aquarium with insect watering gel and food for the crickets. When ready to feed frogs, pick up the paper towel tube and tap the desired amount of crickets into a deli cup with vitamin power. Shake or swirl the cup to dust crickets before feeding them to frogs.

Mites: The Culture Killer

Mites will take over and kill cultures if given the opportunity. Prevention is a must to stop costly culture crashes. Using mite paper is an easy, cost effective way of protecting insect cultures. Mite paper can be purchased from a laboratory supply company or it can be homemade. To make homemade mite paper, purchase a bird mite spray from a local pet retailer. Spray paper towels with the mite spray and allow it to air dry. Once dry, place the paper towels under insect cultures. Homemade and purchased paper should be replaced every 3-4 weeks. This simple prevention can save time and money. If mites take over, an emergency food supply order has to be purchased, which can be quite costly. Checking cultures frequently for mites is also part of the prevention process. If tiny spots can be seen moving around in any culture, then the culture should be disposed of immediately to prevent the spread of mites to other cultures. Mites cannot be irradiated, so constantly managing these pests is vital to having a quality and constant food supply.

Maintaining Cultures

For someone new to the hobby, finding a source for feeder insects and starting cultures should be a high priority. Before obtaining frogs for the first time, a source for purchasing feeder insects should be in place. In addition, a few attempts at culturing insects should be tried. Do not buy dart frogs until after a process and routine for culturing insects has been established. In addition, finding a local source for feeder insects can help reduce costs if emergency cultures need to be purchased.

Once cultures start to produce, it is time to start making new cultures all over again. It is best to produce more cultures than needed. It is important to have extra cultures as a back-up for a culture crash, or to make new cultures. Do not feed off all the insects in a culture. Keeping a portion of insects back allows the insects to continue to reproduce until the culture media is exhausted. Cultures need to be disposed of after 3-4 weeks to manage mites. If a hobbyist keeps several cultures, a rack or shelving system may be needed to store and organize them. The cultures should be arranged from the newest to oldest cultures from the top down, with the newest cultures placed on the top of the rack.

Feeder insects need to be dusted with a calcium and vitamin supplement on a regular basis. This can be accomplished in a few ways. Some hobbyists make a 50-50 mixture of calcium with vitamin D3 and multivitamin that can be purchased from a local pet store. The mixture can be placed in a 32 ounce deli cup. Next, place insects inside the cup and gently swirl them around in the mixture. The vitamins and calcium will attach to the body of the insects. After they are thoroughly coated, the feeders can be added to the terrarium. The dusting can also be done by alternating between calcium and multivitamin during feedings. All in one, vitamin, calcium, and color enhancer supplements are now available for purchase and are the best choice for new hobbyists. When purchasing calcium, make sure it has added vitamin D3 because calcium absorption by the body needs vitamin D3. Paprika from the spice section of a local grocer may also be added to the supplement mix to help with color enhancements in frogs. Supplementing a frog's diet is an important part of preventative health. Frogs that lack proper nutrition will not reproduce, may develop metabolic bone disease, and live a short life.

Albino "Alanis" *Dendrobates tinctorius*

Chapter 4: Acquiring Frogs

Once a decision has been made on what species of dart frog to work with, a terrarium has been built, and a food source has been established, it is time to acquire frogs. Establishing these steps in order is a vital part of a first-time keeper's success in keeping poison dart frogs. Completing these tasks prior to procuring frogs will make it easy to maintain necessary routines required for keeping healthy dart frogs.

There are a variety of different methods available for purchasing poison dart frogs. In today's market, the availability of the internet, trade shows, pet shops, professional breeders, as well as breeders by hobby, provide ample access to these jewels of the rain forest. No matter the chosen method, there are some simple rules to keep in mind when purchasing dart frogs. The main rule is that a hobbyist needs to find out as much information as possible about frogs being considered for purchase. It is also important for a hobbyist to understand the differences between wild caught, farm raised, and captive bred frogs.

Wild caught frogs are taken directly out of their natural habit. Many arrive to the port of entry dehydrated, underfed, and stressed, causing easy transmission of parasitic loads due to their weakened state and unsanitary conditions. Wild caught frogs need to be checked for bacterial and parasitic infections. This will include fecal exams, as well as external exams of the body to make sure there is no damage during transport from country of origin into a reseller's hands. These frogs should undergo quarantine before entering a terrarium. Wild caught frogs are best kept by experienced hobbyists.

Some frogs are considered to be farm raised. Frog farms are areas that may be screened off, or greenhouses, where frogs are raised for the pet trade without harvesting them from the wild. The existence of frog farms, primarily in the country of Panama, is a topic of much debate. Given the condition and quantity of farm raised frogs that enter the U.S., it is likely that many "farm raised" frogs are actually wild caught. Frogs that are farm raised should be treated as if they were wild caught frogs. With an established collection of frogs, any new acquisition should be quarantined from the rest of the collection, especially frogs that are wild caught or of farm-raised origin.

The price of wild caught and farm raised frogs varies and is determined by several factors. Demand, rarity in the hobby, cost per specimen, cost of importation, and profit for the importer all impact cost. These frogs should only be kept by experienced hobbyists. Prices range from $15-$300+ per frog depending on the species.

Captive bred frogs are the offspring of frogs that mate in a captive setting. Their parents may be of wild caught, farm raised, or captive bred origins. Captive bred frogs are susceptible to the same bacterial and parasitic infections as wild caught and farm raised frogs. However, captive bred frogs are less likely to have these infections because they have not had exposure to frogs with these infections. When purchased from a breeder, captive bred frogs typically do not have parasitic infections and are well established. There are some reputable resellers and pet shops that understand the risk of infections and keep their captive bred livestock away from their wild caught livestock, but oftentimes this is not the case. The cost to hobbyists for captive bred frogs is usually similar to the cost of wild caught or farm raised frogs, although some sellers place a higher value on captive bred frogs.

The age of the frog also plays an important role in deciding which frog to purchase. Typically, with captive bred frogs, as the frog ages the price increases. Frogs between the ages of one to three months are often the cheapest, but are also the most fragile. Due to their small size they are more sensitive to changes in their environment. Care for young froglets is difficult, so they are not recommended for the beginning hobbyist. Frogs between the ages of 3 to 6 months are the best value for beginner frog keepers. These frogs are now established with size and are better equipped for environmental changes. At this age, froglets of larger species of dart frogs are unsexable, while some thumbnail species are sexable at six months of age. Most larger species become sexable between 10-14 months of age. A dart frog is usually considered an adult at 12 months of age. Adult frogs tend to be the most expensive frogs to purchase. At times hobbyists will sell tadpoles, which are typically a third of the price of well established frogs. However, tadpoles, like young froglets, are not recommended for beginning hobbyists due to their fragile nature.

It is also important to find out about the lineage of a frog before purchasing. Knowing the lineage of a frog's parents provides a hobbyist with the basic background information needed to intelligently breed frogs in the future. This information will aid in pairing up or matching froglets to a certain importation to reduce the risk of hybridization. Even if a hobbyist is not planning on breeding frogs, it is responsible to keep track of this information in case it is needed in the future.

Before purchasing frogs, do not be afraid to ask questions if any of this information is not provided. After all, the seller is vying for business and should be able to answer inquiries. Remember, information to inquire about includes the age of the frog, the lineage of its parents, and whether the frog is wild caught, farm raised, or captive bred. Depending on the seller, the answers to these questions will vary. Breeders will most often be able to provide the most detailed and accurate information about their frogs. Resellers, jobbers, flippers, or those who are not breeders, such as pet shops, wholesalers, or some trade show or reptile swap sellers, may not know the answers to these questions. These are important questions, so if a seller cannot provide answers about these details they should be avoided.

Where to purchase poison dart frogs is really up to the purchaser. However, in the United States, the location the hobbyist lives in may play a role in the availability of where dart frogs can be purchased. In states like Florida and California it is common to find reptile and amphibian only pet stores, trade shows, and flea market style swaps where reptiles and amphibians are bought and sold. Check area and state listings on the Internet to see if there is a reptile or amphibian sale in a specific area. Hobbyists may be surprised to find an event relatively close to where they live. While attending a sale, hobbyists will encounter both breeders and resellers. Do not be afraid to ask questions as both wild caught and captive bred frogs are commonly available.

There are various sources for purchasing frogs on the Internet. Using popular search engines, it is possible to find forum groups, breeders, and classifieds dedicated to reptiles and amphibians. Many hobbyists sell their offspring on online forums, and professional breeders may sponsor the forum and have links from the forum to their websites. Popular online classifieds are another way of finding professional breeders and hobbyists that are selling. When purchasing on the Internet, as always use precaution. Again, do not be afraid to ask questions. The questions stated earlier are just beginning inquiries to make sure the buyer feels secure about the purchase. It is appropriate to find out if there are any guarantees, how the frogs will be shipped, and any other details the buyer feels necessary. Many professional breeders will already have common questions answered in their terms of sale on their website. Also, be sure to use a traceable payment method such as a credit card, checking account, or an internet-based payment system in the event a dispute needs to be made. Be sure to provide the seller with all necessary personal information needed to complete the transaction, including a phone number to be reached at. Shipping companies often require the receiver's phone number with live shipments in case of delay or other error.

Shipping is done using insulated boxes. These boxes contain a Styrofoam insert that slides into the box. Frogs are placed in deli cups with plant cuttings.

Shipping is required for some purchases. One of the benefits of attending a trade show or purchasing from a local pet store is that frogs are available for choosing and the buyer can leave with them the same day. Purchasing online may require the frogs to be shipped if the breeder is not in the buyer's immediate area. Shipping is done using one of the many commercially available shipping companies. The standard method is next day air AM service, but this varies depending on the company. Frogs are shipped using Styrofoam insulated boxes. Depending on the weather, heating or cooling packs will be added to keep frogs at the optimal temperature. The frogs are placed inside of a deli cup with either a moistened paper towel or sphagnum moss and fresh cut leaves from the terrarium. The cup is placed in the center of the box and newspaper is wedged snuggly around the container so it is not jostled during transportation. Be sure to check the seller's terms for guarantees on live arrival and how it is handled if the animal arrives deceased. Reputable sellers guarantee live arrival, so do not risk buying from those who do not offer this guarantee. In addition, get all available contact information from the seller. Do not settle for just an email address. If the package is rerouted, delayed, or lost the seller's information will be needed to get the problem corrected.

Calling *O. pumilio* "Cayo de Aqua", many wild caught frogs begin calling after being introduced into habitat.

Chapter 5: Quarantine and Health

Any newly acquired animal should go through proper quarantine and hygiene practices. Even captive bred animals from reputable breeders should undergo a period of quarantine in a separate area before being introduced to a general collection. Best practice will protect the animals, an established collection, and the buyer's investment.

Handling amphibians should be kept to a minimum. When handling and transporting is required, care should be given to reduce direct contact. A soft fish dip net can be used to help catch frogs. A clear cup or vial can also be used to catch and transport frogs. Disposable spoons can be placed in front of frogs and many times they will walk on the spoon and the frogs can be moved. If direct contact is needed, latex or rubber gloves rinsed in amphibian safe water can be worn.

O. pumilio undergoing a visual inspection using a spoon.

When adding new additions to a collection, they should be the last of the animals cared for in a hobbyist's daily routines. Any cage furnishings should not be shared or reused unless properly disinfected. Disinfecting furnishings and housing containers can be accomplished by using a 10% bleach solution with a 1:10 ratio of bleach to water. ¾ cup of non-scented bleach to a gallon of tap water is an easy measure to follow to create a 10% bleach solution. Wipe down nonporous items with this solution and allow items to sit for 10-15 minutes before rinsing in hot water. Plants that are clean of all soil can be soaked in the same solution for 30 minutes and then rinsed. Please note, this can kill some plants so use discretion. When moving from tank to tank, properly sanitize hands by washing them with anti-microbial soap for 30 seconds, then rinse thoroughly.

"Black" *Dendrobates auratus* in a simple quarantine set-up.

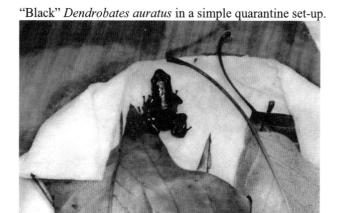

Separate housing should be used as a quarantine area before introducing frogs to their new habitat. Quarantine should last a minimum of 30 days and last as long as needed. Frogs that are known to have issues should be quarantined for a minimum of 45 days. Some frogs may need to be quarantined for a year or longer to ensure they are healthy. Visible concerns may include physical issues such as rub nose or open wounds. Rub nose is caused by repeated hits to the snout when frogs jump in cramped quarters. Fecals should also be done to ensure there is not a hidden parasite issue. Fecals should be completed by a veterinarian familiar with amphibians. The quarantine area should be separated from the general collection, and in an ideal world, in a separate facility. These habitats should be kept simple and cleaned on a routine basis, every, or every other, day. Cleaning should be completed using the 1:10 bleach to water ratio. Substrate can be damp white paper towels or long fiber sphagnum moss. Substrate should be disposed of at each cleaning. When treating for internal parasites, daily cleaning is required during the treatment phase. Animals should be returned to a clean, sanitized container after treatment. If an animal is being treated for infection or wounds, quarantine should not be ended until the infection is gone and wounds are completely healed.

190 oz container set up for. O. pumilio quarantine. Film canisters and leaf litter aid in the reduction of stress.

Observations are a crucial part of quarantine. Noticing symptoms and signs of health issues allows for quick treatment. Fecal exams should be done during this time. The second week of quarantine is a good time to a collect fresh stool samples for testing. A good stool should look like a little sausage and be brown to dark brown in coloration. There may be some red coloration from the eyes of the flies frogs consume. To collect a sample, use a plastic spoon to extract feces from the terrarium. It is best to find a freshly defecated sample. Once collected, place the feces on a damp paper towel and place it in a plastic zipping sandwich bag. Samples need to arrive at a facility to be tested within 48 hours. If sending to a lab or an out of area veterinarian, next day or second day air service is required. Newly acquired animals should also be checked for any physical imperfections and abnormalities. After these checks are completed, daily observations should be taken. Observers should look for diarrhea or no stool, lethargic movements, poor color, weight loss, little growth or weight gain (juveniles), and poor appetite. Any issues should be immediately addressed by a professional.

Treatments requiring pharmaceuticals should be administered after a consultation and the consent of a veterinarian. When possible, use a veterinarian who is a member of the Association of Reptilian and Amphibian Veterinarians (ARAV). Panacur® (Fenbendazole) is a popular treatment for gastrointestinal parasites (Nematodes). A common dosage in amphibians is oral dosages dusted on food given 1-3 times a week for 3 weeks. Ivermectin is another broad-spectrum pharmaceutical often used on Nematodes resistant to Fenbendazole, but it has a much smaller range of safety. However, this drug can be given as a bath instead of dusting. The bath dosage is created by diluting 10 mg of Ivermectin into 1000 mL of water. Soak the frog in a shallow bath of the dilution for 60-120 minutes once a week for three weeks. Protozoal infections and bacterial infections are often treated with Flagyl® (Metronidazole). Flagyl® has shown effectiveness against Flagellates, Protozoans, and Amoebas. Again, this treatment is done orally dusted on food 1-3 times a week for 3 weeks. Injectable metronidazole, 5mg/mL, can be used by placing a drop on the back of the frog once a week for

3 weeks. Fish grade metronidazole has been used for a 5-10 minute soaking, with unsubstantiated results. Diagnoses of the infections mentioned above are discovered through a fecal exam. Physical symptoms such as lethargic behavior, skinny appearance, or bloating can be observable warning signs to warrant a fecal exam to test for these infections.

Physical injuries such as nose rub can be treated with topical treatments. The most common method of treatment is triple action antibacterial cream. Most open wounds should be treated with triple action antibacterial cream applied directly to the wound. Lesions can be treated using Silver sulfadiazine cream. Physical injuries can also be treated with a cotton swap

The injury on the head of this *Oophaga pumilio* is common among recent imports. Treatment during quarantine is needed.

dipped in Methylene Blue, and applied to the wound. The wound will take on a blue coloration during treatment. Methylene Blue can be found in the fish section of pet stores. Additional treatments can be done as needed.

Unfortunately, euthanasia may be needed to end the suffering of an animal if their injuries are untreatable. Being endothermic, freezing a reptile or amphibian was once an acceptable euthanasia practice. However, this is no longer the case. If euthanasia is required for an amphibian, the most humane method is to anesthetize the animal prior to euthanasia. The easiest way to accomplish this task is to apply *Benzocaine* to the belly of an amphibian. *Benzocaine* is a pain killer that can be found in Orajel® and other toothache medications. To anesthetize a frog, apply a small amount of this topical medication to the underside of an amphibian. To euthanize the frog, apply a second dose of the medication to the back of the frog after it has been anesthetized. A more complicated way to anesthetize a frog is to soak the animal in a shallow dish of 25 mL of 80 proof vodka diluted with 175 mL of water. To euthanize the frog, place it in a dish of straight vodka after the frog has been anesthetized. All treatments should be done on the consult of a veterinarian.

Chytrid

Hobbyists should be aware of a fungus that is rapidly affecting amphibians. *Batrachochytrium dendrobatidis, Bd,* is a type of chytrid fungus discovered in 1999 that attacks the skin of amphibians and has been found on amphibian's skin for several years prior to its discovery. This fungus is more commonly called chytrid and Chytridiomycosis when affecting the amphibians. The fungus allows the buildup of keratin on the outer layer of the skin of amphibians. Amphibians drink through their skin and some even breathe through their skin. The buildup of keratin stops these processes. This epidemic is almost worldwide, and is responsible for killing entire populations of amphibians in the wild.

A few species of amphibians are resistant to the fungus, but are still carriers. Chytrid is spread through the transfer of its zoospores. Zoospores are reproductive cells of fungi. The zoospores are transferred through moisture. An infected animal can transfer the fungus through direct contact or contact with moist caging, furnishings, or water from its habitat. Porous objects may hide pockets of zoospores. Great care needs to be given not to transfer zoospores to healthy thriving animals. Some symptoms can be seen in amphibians with chytrid. Excessive shedding, reddish coloration, or discoloration may be observed. However, only through polymerase chain reaction (PCR) testing can a diagnosis be confirmed. This testing requires a laboratory.

Chytrid is treatable in captive situations with Itraconazole baths or other anti-fungal medications. An over the counter anti-fungal, Lamasil AT® spray, has shown successful treatment. The active ingredient in Lamasil AT®, Terbinafine hydrochloride, has been shown to treat chytrid. Dilutions at 0.05-0.10 mL of the anti-fungal Terbinafine hydrochloride can be used to soak a frog for 5 minutes a day over 6-8 days. When using Lamasil AT®, an easy dilution to use is 10 mL of Lamasil AT® to 200 mL of water to soak a frog for 5 minutes per day for a minimum of 10 days. Disposal or glass pipettes should be used to help fully cover the frog with the medicated solution during treatments. After treatments, frogs should be returned to a clean, sanitized quarantine container. A fresh dilution needs to be made daily when providing treatments. The container the medication is administered in needs to be cleaned between treatments using a bleach solution (1 cup bleach to 1 gallon water). All treatment regiments should be done on the consult of a veterinarian.

Chapter 6: Breeding

During dart frog reproduction males call out for females. Females respond by laying eggs. The eggs are often laid on leaves, or another egg laying site. Most dart frogs lay very few eggs, ranging from 2-8 on average, although some species have been known to lay larger clutches. Males fertilize the eggs within 1-2 days. After fertilization, eggs typically hatch within 12-14 days. During this time, the embryo changes from a blackish, grayish dot to more of a tadpole form within the egg. The male frogs of these species care for their offspring by watching over the eggs. Once tadpoles hatch, the male carries them on his back to a water source. Normally this is the end of the parental care of the tadpoles. In some dart frog species known as obligated egg feeders, the female watches over the eggs and carries the tadpoles to water. She then lays eggs in the water for the tadpoles to eat. The eggs are necessary for the tadpoles' development into frogs. Dart frogs are really the only amphibians that play a part in raising their young.

The breeding of poison dart frogs in captivity plays a crucial part in the conservation and continuance of the many species in the hobby. By breeding frogs in captivity, hobbyists reduce the amount of animals taken from the wild. In addition, many counties have shut down their borders to the exportation of flora and fauna so breeding frogs in captivity ensures these animals remain in the hobby. For example, "Blue Jeans" were once a common frog in the United States due to their large importations, but very few were bred in captivity. When Costa Rica shut down its borders to exportations in the early 90's, the number of these frogs in the hobby decreased. If more hobbyists had successfully bred "Blue Jeans" in captivity this decrease in numbers might not have been as severe. The importance of captive breeding can certainly be seen with this morph of *pumilio*.

Breeding dart frogs in captivity begins with a mature male-female pair. Obtaining adult sexed pairs can be difficult. Sexed pairs of common species can sometimes be purchased from large breeders. Typically, they run 3-4 times the price of buying froglets. Many people elect to buy a group of froglets and play the odds of obtaining a pair. The following chart shows the odds of obtaining a sexed pair based on the number of froglets purchased:

Number of Froglets Purchased	1	2	3	4	5	6	7	8
Odds of a Sexed Pair	0%	50%	75%	88%	94%	97%	98%	99%

When electing to buy a group of froglets, keep in mind it may take 10 or more months for frogs to be properly sexed and another six months before they reproduce. Without having a proven breeding pair, calling is the only true way of sexing a male. Other indicators can help determine the sex of dart frogs. In larger species, except for *Oophaga pumilio*, the males are smaller in length and have large front toe pads. The enlarged toe pads of males often take on a heart shape. Females have smaller toe pads and their body is longer in length. Many will have a plump belly indicating they are gravid. The existence of plump fatty tissue near the rear legs and a rather large, fat stomach are often signs of a female dart frog. The difference in physical size between males and females is known as sexual dimorphism. The pictures on page 51 show stereotypical male-female pairs of *Dendrobates tinctorius* and *auratus*.

Male Dwarf Cobalt
Dendrobates tinctorius,
notice the enlarged front
toe pads. This is a
stereotypical look of a
male *tinctorius.*

Below is an adult pair of
tincs. The female (left) is
larger and has fatty sides,
while the male (right) is
shorter and slender.

(Left)The shorter,
slender male
(Right) Female
with larger and
fatty sides
"Bronze and
Green"
D. auratus

After a male-female pair of dart frogs has been acquired, be sure to prepare an egg laying site in the frogs' enclosure. A popular egg laying site, especially for larger species such as *D. auratus*, *D. tinctorius*, or *Phyllobates,* is beneath a coconut hut that can be purchased for around $5 at a local pet shop. Hobbyists can easily make their own huts as well. Coconuts are around $3-5 at a local grocer. Instructions for making coconut huts, and coconut water dishes, can be found in the "Additional Notes" section. Inside the tank, position the coconut hut on a solid foundation and under each hut place an open petri dish. Petri dishes can be purchased from an online frog store or at a local hobby and science shop. The frogs will breed within the hut and lay eggs on the petri dish.

Once the eggs are laid, it is the responsibility of the hobbyist to check if the eggs are fertile. Carefully remove the petri dish and observe the eggs. Fertile eggs have a jelly like coating over them, while unfertilized eggs look flat and lack the coating. If the eggs appear to be unfertile, return them to the tank because the male may still fertilize them. Check again the next day and if the eggs are still unfertile, remove the eggs from the tank and throw them away. After two days, the male has lost interest and will not fertilize the eggs. If the eggs are fertile, remove the petri dish from the tank and use a spray bottle to add water to the petri dish containing the eggs. Add just enough water to keep the eggs moist, but do not submerge them. Place the lid on the petri dish to control evaporation. Place the petri dish in a safe place at room temperature where it can remain flat for approximately two weeks as the embryo develops into a tadpole. Removing fertilized eggs from the tank is often advantageous because it eliminates risk factors that could destroy the eggs. For example, frogs may purposefully or inadvertently stomp out the eggs. Removing the eggs also makes it easier for a hobbyist to monitor and cultivate development. After removing the petri dish from the tank, remember to replace the dish that was removed with a new dish.

The darkened and extra skin on the throat of the right *O. pumilio* indicates this *pumilio* has been calling. This is a wild caught "Cristobal."

Other egg laying sites may also be utilized by frogs. Substrate such as leaf litter consisting of oak, magnolia, or almond leaves provides hiding and egg laying areas. Live plants such as pothos or bromeliads may provide a place for frogs to lay eggs. If eggs are laid on leaf litter or plants, the eggs can safely be extracted from the tank by cutting the leaf the eggs are on to size and placing the leaf, with the eggs on it, in a petri dish. Some species may lay eggs on the side of the glass. These eggs can be removed gently with a razor blade. Carefully slide the razor blade under the eggs and transfer them to a petri dish, taking care not to rupture the eggs. Another potential egg laying site for thumbnail species, and smaller frogs such as *pumilio*, is a 35mm film canister. Use a suction cup to secure the film canister to the terrarium glass. Drill a hole in the side of the film canister in order to attach a suction cup to it. Since frogs prefer to lay their eggs in moist environments, position the canister on the side of the terrarium at an upward angle to allow water to collect inside the bottom of the canister. To remove eggs from a film canister, detach the canister from the side of the terrarium and place it inside a deli cup with a shallow pool of water. Place the canister on its side to allow water to reach the eggs. Eggs may become unattached from the canister after some time and can be gently flushed out with water into a petri dish. If the eggs remain attached to the canister the tadpoles will develop without issue inside the film canister. It is alright to remove eggs from an enclosure for the majority of dart frog species, but do not remove the eggs of *O. pumilio*.

Rather than remove dart frog eggs from a terrarium, in some situations it is advisable to leave eggs in the tank. The genus *Oophaga*, belong to a group of frogs known as obligated egg feeders. The tadpoles of these species must receive a protein from their mothers' eggs to feed on or they will not develop. All obligated egg feeder eggs and tadpoles must be raised by their parents and therefore must be left in the tank. From the author's experience, it is also recommended that beginner hobbyists allow parents of thumbnail species to raise their tadpoles as well. Thumbnail species are small and as they develop the eggs and tadpoles will be very small. Allowing parents to raise the tadpoles is naturalistic and gives froglets the best chance to grow to maturity. However, frogs often will not take care of all their tadpoles, so do not expect all eggs that are laid to develop into tadpoles. This method yields a smaller amount of froglets than if all the eggs were successfully extracted and raised, however accomplishing this task is very difficult. Terrariums need to be well seeded with microfauna as froglets are often too small to eat fruit flies. For a beginner working with thumbnail species, the advantages of allowing parents to naturally rear their young outweigh the possibility of

Egg Development

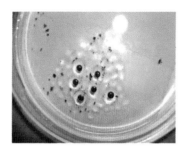

Freshly laid eggs,
Dendrobates tinctorius.

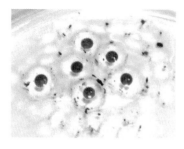

After 1-2 days, the embryos
start to turn light gray and a
line forms across the center.

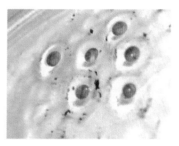

At 3-4 days old the body becomes
more visible in definition.

At 5-7 days the body of the
embryo is now visible.

At 9-10 days the embryo is
almost ready to hatch.

After eggs are fertilized it
typically takes 12-14 days for
tadpoles to hatch.

fewer overall froglets. It is recommended that a hobbyist gain experience rearing larger species of dart frogs first before attempting to raise thumbnail species.

Raising Tadpoles

Raising new tadpoles is just as rewarding as keeping frogs. If eggs hatch in the tank, male dart frogs will care for the tadpoles by transporting them to water. Some species require extended parental care, such as *Oophaga pumilio*, and must remain in the terrarium. Keepers who choose to artificially raise their tadpoles will need to be vigilant in care. When raising tadpoles several considerations need to be addressed. Monitoring housing, water quality, and feeding for these new additions is essential to yielding fruitful development into froglets.

There are several methods to choose from when deciding how to house tadpoles. A common rule to remember is that simplicity is the best route to take when deciding on a housing technique for tadpoles. One housing method is to use completely separate units for each tadpole. Using 16 oz deli cups, one tadpole can be housed in each cup. *Dendrobatidae* tadpoles can be cannibalistic, and individual housing is the only way to completely prevent cannibalism. The water level in the cup does not need to be exact, but the tadpole needs to have enough water to swim in. Also keep in mind that the more water there is in the cup, the less often the water will need to be changed. Keep the lid on the deli cup to control temperature and water evaporation. Another housing technique is to use a bolt and screw organizer from the local hardware store. This method also controls cannibalism. The organizer keeps tadpoles separated into individual compartments within the container while reducing the amount of space individual deli cups would use. This is the most ideal set-up for housing thumbnail species. Larger species such as *tinctorius* can be housed in a group setting, although this is not a recommended method for thumbnails. Using a sweater box sized plastic box, 7 tadpoles can be housed in one unit. Make sure not to overcrowd tadpoles housed in groups, and keep them well fed. The tadpoles will become cannibalistic through competition if they are not well fed. Once a housing decision has been made, the removal of tadpoles from the petri dish to the containers is a sensitive step that must be taken. The easiest way to transfer a tadpole without harm is to use a kitchen turkey baster to suck the tadpole up and push it out into its new environment.

Water quality is another major variable that needs to be monitored in order to keep tadpoles healthy. To begin with, keep it simple by using the water mixture that is already being used for adult dart frogs, as described in Chapter 2. For tadpoles, add an extra step to the process to create a "tadpole tea." Soak magnolia, Indian almond, and/or oak leaves in water to create a tea of sorts. The purpose of the "tea" is to help create acidic water, enriched with tannins to protect tadpoles from fungal and bacterial infections. Another, perhaps easier, way to create "tadpole tea" is to add a black water, or peat, extract to water. This extract can be purchased from a local pet shop. This is a common water treatment that is commercially designed to create an Amazon like water quality for discus and other tropical fish, but it works well for dart frog tadpoles. The

Tadpole tea and simple ingredients.

water temperature for tadpoles should be maintained at around 75°F (24°C). Higher temperatures lead to faster metamorphosis and smaller froglets. Faster morphing can cause serious health risks to tadpoles and froglets. Lower temperatures have no ill effect, but it will take a little longer for tadpoles to morph into froglets.

Water in the tadpoles' housing should be changed about twice weekly if tadpoles are reared in groups. A simple method of changing water is to pour new water into the container to displace old water to complete a partial water change. A partial water change is preferable to an entire water change because a full water change may alter water chemistry too much. The new water should be kept in the same room as the tadpoles for several hours. This ensures it reaches the same water temperature tadpoles are currently living in before a partial water change is completed. If water changes are not done, the results can be lethal. Tadpoles can produce a growth regulation hormone when kept in a group setting. This hormone slows the growth of the other tadpoles, but frequent water changes reduce hormone levels. Water also needs to be changed in order to rid the container of waste and uneaten food. Tadpoles that are housed individually in 16 oz deli cups or bolt and screw organizers do not require as frequent water changes, however keepers may elect to complete partial water changes more often to rid the container of waste.

Providing an effective food source for tadpoles is a necessity for which there are several different solutions. A popular food choice is a high grade premium tropical fish food of a powered spirulina diet. A tropical flake fish food with spirulina already added can also be used. A natural food choice is java moss, *Vesicularia dubyana*, an Asian moss that tadpoles will feed on. This can be fed to tadpoles by cutting small strands of the moss and placing it in tadpole cups in addition to flake food. Java moss is extremely easy to grow, which makes it an easy to maintain food source, although it quickly becomes overgrown when used in aquariums. Indian almond leaves, or leaf parts, may also be added to tadpole containers as an additional food, and to increase the tannin levels. Another food choice is human grade spirulina and chlorella purchased from a local health food store. Tablets of these algae are ground together to form a diet suitable for the small mouths of tadpoles. Tadpole bite pellets can also be used for thumbnail species, but from the author's experience a plankton tablet with spirulina is a better choice. Tadpoles should be fed 3-4 times a week.

Raising Froglets

From the moment a tadpole hatches from the egg to the development of its front legs, it takes an average of three months for a tadpole to become a froglet. Once tadpoles have their front and hind legs, they are ready to be transferred to a rearing container. Rectangular disposable food storage containers work well for this purpose. Add water to the container and place it on a shelf at a slanted angle to force the water to collect at one end. Moistened strands of sphagnum peat moss may be placed in the elevated end of the container, which is not full of water, to create a land area for the froglet. During this stage, the tadpole will not feed until it fully becomes a froglet. Once a froglet's tail is completely absorbed it can be placed in its temporary home. Temporary housing is needed due to the small size of the froglet, and will allow for observation, feeding, and growth. Placing a newly morphed froglet into an adult terrarium will be fatal. Disposable food storage containers or 190 oz deli cup style containers can be used for temporary homes for froglets, housing up to 3-4 froglets together. However, two months after a tadpole has morphed into a froglet, there should be no more than two frogs per disposable container. If an aquarium is used as a rearing habitat, as a rule, there is enough space to raise one froglet for every gallon of tank space. Pay close attention to the growth rate of froglets. Those that are growing quickly should be moved to a different container with similar sized frogs. Moistened sphagnum peat moss can be used for ground cover with 1-2 inches of oak, magnolia, or almond leaves included for hiding areas. Some hobbyists add live plants to their temporary housing enclosures. Feeding of froglets should be done daily. Froglets are very small and need a small food source such as springtails, isopods, and *D.melanogaster*. Containers should be cleaned before being reused and spot cleaning should be done weekly. Moss should be replaced monthly. A shallow water dish needs to be provided for soaking. Be sure the water depth is not deeper than what the froglets can stand in, otherwise they can drown. Once froglets are about 4-5 months old they can be introduced into their regular terrarium habitat.

Male D. tinctorius "Azereus" transporting a tadpole

Chapter 7: Conservation

These beautiful and interesting jewels known as dart frogs may soon no longer be commonplace in the wild. Devastating changes are occurring across the world. According to the Global Amphibian Assessment, there are approximately 6,000 known species of amphibians. As many as 165 amphibian species may already be extinct. With at least 43% of all species of amphibians declining in population, this is the largest extinction since the dinosaurs.

Dart frogs are hard to monitor because of the remote locations they are found in, however there is one environmental factor known as the *Bd* chytrid fungus which has one of the biggest impacts of all in terms of declining amphibian populations. The warmer temperature of earth, caused by global warming, is considered to be one of the causes of the rapid growth of the fungus. The sad reality is that many amphibian species may be wiped from the face of the earth as a result of the fungus. A group of animals that has been on earth for thousands of years may become missing for future generations.

Other environmental issues, such as reduction of habitat, are negatively affecting dart frogs and other inhabitants of their fragile ecosystems. Sections of rain forest continue to be cut down for timber that is used for construction and paper products. Without this area, several species of animals become homeless. The cleared land is then used for farming. However, the rain forest contains soil that is poor in nutrients so farms can fail within a few years. Other human interaction has a negative effect as well. People use chemicals in their homes that are not always necessary, but are harmful to the environment. These chemicals leak into water sources contaminating the water and effectively killing wildlife.

As a hobbyist, there are some preventative measures that can be taken to preserve amphibians' natural environment. It is always best practice to leave a found animal alone. Also, never release a pet or plants that were in an aquarium into the wild. This is not only irresponsible, but illegal. The animal, even if it is native, may have a disease and the plants may be a carrier of the disease. Releasing a pet may have other consequences too. Introducing a new species that has no natural predators means the animal may have the opportunity to become invasive. This means the species can grow rapidly and take over the natural habitat of another species and push that species out. An exotic invasive species may also feed on the native species and lead to the loss of a species. Actions like these have enticed several communities and states to ban the ownership of exotic wildlife. Being a responsible hobbyist promotes the continuance of the hobby and captive pet trade, thus leading to captive breeding and overall conservation of dart frogs.

Additional Notes

Fruit Fly Media Recipe (for fruit fly cultures)
Simple Formula
Works for *Drosophila melanogaster* and *hydei*

This formula has proven to be successful for several years. Products in this recipe can be purchased from among a local grocer, health food store, or, for reduced cost, at a bulk food store. This recipe makes enough media for 4-6 cultures.

5 cups of instant potato flakes
¼ cup of powdered sugar
1 teaspoon of baker's yeast
¼ cup of brewer's yeast (from a health food store)
50% water and 50% white vinegar mixture

For the water/vinegar mixture there is no exact measure of liquid, but an applesauce like consistency is ultimately desired for the completed mixture. Typically start using a cup of water to a cup of vinegar. If more liquid needs to be included, add more water because *Drosophila hydei* are sensitive to vinegar.

Stir all ingredients together until a thinner consistency of mashed potatoes, or an applesauce like mixture, is achieved. Ingredients can be mixed together by hand, or using a mixer. If it appears too much liquid has been used, then add more potato flakes. Left over mixed media can be frozen and reused.

Using a mold inhibitor is optional. If a mold inhibitor is used, pure methyl paraben is recommended. Sources of this product can be found online. If methyl paraben is used, vinegar is no longer needed. Add 2 teaspoons of methyl paraben for every 5 cups of potato flakes. Add water until the desired consistency for the media is achieved.

DIY (do-it-yourself) Insect Culturing Cups

Raising and culturing feeders from home is a cost effective way of managing a collection. Insect culturing cups are needed for fruit fly and bean weevil production. Commercially available cups are available, however making cups is simple. The following steps demonstrate how to create insect culturing cups.

Materials:
excelsior   scissors
32 oz deli cups and lids   paper towels
fruit fly media (for fruit fly cultures)   coffee filters
black-eyed peas (for bean weevil cultures)

Step 1: The Lid
32 ounce cups and lids can be purchased from a local bulk food supply store. Carefully cut a hole in the lid to allow for ventilation, similar to the lid pictured below.

Step 2: Escape Proof Covering

After making a hole in the lid, an escape proof vent needs to be made to cover this opening. The best product to use is paper towels. Fold a paper towel in half lengthwise (hot dog fold). Then fold the towel again to make an approximate square. Unfold the last crease and cut the paper towel along the fold into two sections. This creates two covers for two cultures. Do not try to save money by cutting the paper towel into fourths to create four covers. Fruits flies will escape if only a single layer of paper towel is used! Coffee filters may be substituted for paper towels, but a double layer of filters must also be used.

  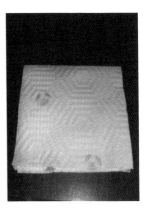

Step 3: Finishing Touches

Add 1½ -2 inches of media to the bottom of the deli cup. For bean weevils, use dried black-eyed peas for media at a depth of 1-1½ inches, making sure that some of the peas come from a preexisting culture. Also add a loosely crumpled up coffee filter so the weevils have something to crawl on. Add a couple dozen weevils from a preexisting culture. For fruit flies, use the media from the recipe provided in the previous section. To support the flies, be sure to add coffee filters and excelsior.

Fold two filters into quarters and insert them into the media across from each other along the sides of the cup. Fill the deli cup ¾ full with loose excelsior. Place the excelsior between the filters. Excelsior can be purchased at a craft or hobby store. Add about 2-3 dozen flies from a preexisting culture. After insects are in the deli cup, place the paper towel cover and lid on top of the deli cup to seal the container. The final picture below shows what finished fruit fly cultures look like after everything has come together.

DIY Coconut Hut or Water Bowl

The coconut hut plays a critical role in the reproduction of poison dart frogs by providing a place for shelter, security, and an egg laying site. As an artistic addition to any terrarium, a coconut hut can also be turned upside down to be used as a naturalistic water dish. By following these steps, hobbyists will be able to make their own coconut huts. Please adhere to all safety instructions on power tools that may be used and wear safety glasses when creating a coconut hut.

Materials:

coconut	hole saw 1.5"-2"
drill	large spoon or screw driver
large pot for boiling	file or sandpaper
saw (hand or table)	table vice (optional)
¾" drill bit	safety glasses

Step 1: Obtain a coconut from a local grocer. Create 1-2 holes in the coconut in order to drain the milk. Using the ¾" drill bit, drill two holes, one at each end of the coconut. Instead of a drill, a screwdriver can be used to pierce the coconut to create the holes. If creating a water bowl, drill the holes in the center of the coconut rather than the two ends. After the holes are made, allow the coconut milk to drain out.

Step 2: If creating a water dish, skip this step. To create a hut, use the hole saw to drill a hole in the center of the coconut. To hold the coconut in place, hobbyists can put the coconut between their feet, or use a table vice. If a hole saw is not available, a hobbyist may skip this step for the time being and can instead cut an upside down "V" into the cleaned coconut shell that remains after Step 4.

Step 3: Using a hand or table saw carefully cut the coconut in half. If creating a hut instead of a water dish, be sure to cut the coconut in half through the center of the hole that was created using the hole saw. If using a table saw, the blade only needs to be raised about an inch.

Step 4: After the coconut is cut into two halves, rinse both haves in water to remove excess debris. Next, boil the coconut halves for 10-15 minutes to loosen the meat of the coconut. Remove the halves from the boiling water and use a screw driver to pry around the edge of the coconut and the shell. Be sure to pry completely around the coconut. Once finished, carefully pry the 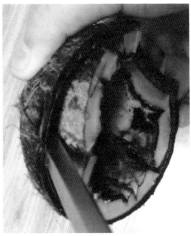 coconut meat from the shell using a large spoon or screw driver. If a hobbyist is lucky, the entire contents will come out all at once.

Step 5: Inspect around the coconut shell that remains and look for sharp edges. Sand or file down these areas. Once finished, install in the terrarium.

DIY Background: Clay

One of the rewarding experiences of keeping poison dart frogs is creating an aesthetically pleasing terrarium to display in the home or office. Clay backgrounds are easy to create and a very popular design choice.

Step 1: Obtain the main ingredient for the clay background. Cheaper store brand cat litters consist of ground clay pieces. When soaked in water the litter becomes moldable clay. Check the ingredients and select a cat litter without additives in the bag.

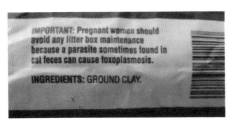

This label shows only ground clay in the ingredients.

Step 2: Place a desired amount of clay in a 5 gallon pail in preparation to mix the clay. About 30 lbs of clay is needed to complete an 18×18×24 inch terrarium background. Use a consistent scoop to help measure the amount of clay used.

Step 3: Add water to the clay. Use a paint stirrer or other sturdy item to mix the water and clay to a desired consistency that can be squeezed like play-dough. If the mix is too wet then add more litter. When adding water, it may need to sit for a few hours to be fully absorbed by the clay.

Step 4: Milled sphagnum peat moss needs to be added to create a naturalistic look and help create a constancy that will allow the clay to stick to the back of the terrarium. For every 2-3  scoops of litter, add one scoop of milled sphagnum peat moss. More water may be needed to maintain a pliable product.

Step 5: Building the background is fairly easy. Wearing disposable gloves, build a base at the bottom of the back wall of the tank that is wider than the desired background. Slowly add clay until the back of the terrarium is covered with the clay mix. Once the back is covered, fingerprints and hand imprints can be smoothed out using hands, stone, or another object that  leaves the desired look. Film canisters can be pressed into the clay if the tank is used for thumbnails or *pumilio*.

Step 6: After all the clay has been added to create the background, plants can be added directly into the clay. Planting is as easy as pressing the plant's roots into the soft clay. For plants with a larger root tap, use a plastic spoon or a finger to poke a hole into the clay large enough to place the plant, and then press clay around the base of the plant to hold it firmly in place. If the clay becomes too hard, mist the background with water to make it more malleable.

Drainage Layer Using Egg Crate

When building the drainage layer of a terrarium, a popular option besides LECA is the use of egg crate. Egg crate can be purchased in the lighting section or drop ceiling section of a local hardware store. These steps can be substituted for Step 2 and 3 of the basic terrarium design instructions in Chapter 2.

Step 1: Determine the dimensions needed to create a false bottom using egg crate. The egg crate will be inserted into the bottom of the aquarium or terrarium, so keep in mind it will need to be smaller than the dimensions of the terrarium. The gaps around the egg crate base will need to be filled with gravel or LECA to prevent standing water. If these gaps are not filled, then the drainage layer is not complete and there is a risk frogs could drown in the water that collects. Once the dimensions have been chosen, check to see if they align with the rows of egg crate. Use smaller dimensions if the exact dimensions do not align.

Step 2: Cutting egg crate is simple. Using a pair of pliers, snip the plastic pieces that separate the desired amount of crate from the larger unit to create the base, or surface of the platform. Once completed, file the sharp edges. Diagonal pliers work best for a clean cut. Needle nose pliers are just as effective, but cause the plastic pieces to fracture when cut.

Step 3: The base needs supports to elevate it and allow water to drain to the bottom of the tank. Typically a 1½-2½ inch layer of egg crate, a height of 2-3 squares, is used, but this varies by terrarium design depending on how tall the hobbyist wants to make the drainage layer. Cut the crate to meet the length and width of the base. Connect the sections to the base using zip ties.

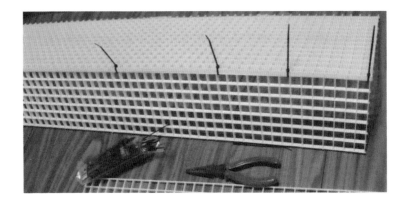

Step 4: Add additional support across the base so it does not collapse under the weight of the substrate and any other décor that may be added. If a bulkhead is not used on this terrarium PVC pipe can be used again to create an access to allow the use of a siphon. Small holes can be drilled into the PVC pipe to zip tie the pipe to the egg crate base.

Step 5: Install the false bottom in the terrarium. Cover the egg crate with landscaping fabric or fiberglass screen. Fill the area around the covered egg crate base with gravel or LECA. Place another layer of fabric or screen over the base and gravel/LECA. To finish the tank, continue with the rest of the steps of the simple terrarium design.

If a water feature is desired, do not create a square or rectangular base but create an irregular shape to allow an area for a small "pond." Even though the majority of the base has smaller dimensions than the terrarium, be sure to extend the portion sectioning off the "pond" to the edge of the glass.

Use landscaping fabric to cover the egg crate base with the cut out water feature. Use LECA to fill the gaps around the edges.

Add a second layer of landscaping fabric covering the entire base to allow substrate to be added to and to plant the tank.

Finish the terrarium by planting and adding leaf litter. Rinsed aquarium gravel is used in the water feature area. Slate is used to create a boundary between the "pond" and the terrarium soil. This tank is designed for *O. pumilio*, "Blue Jeans" Costa Rica locality.

Commercially Available Terrariums: Adapted for Dart Frogs

Hobbyists are no longer restricted to the confines of standard aquariums. However, commercially available terrariums do require some modifications to stop the escape of fruit flies. The front vents can be sealed using silicone, but the author does not make this modification. The only modification the author makes is in the lid.

Step 1: The lid is the main part that requires modifications.

Terrariums are built with screen lids, which will allow fruit flies to escape. Using a screw driver, pull the rubber spline off. Once the spline is removed, the screen will pop out, although some force may be needed. If UV lighting is used, only remove one panel of screen. This can only be done on Ex-Terra® terrariums as the Zoo Med® terrariums only have one large screen lid.

Step 2: Once the screen is removed, it can be replaced with glass. Custom cut glass

will be required. Clean the lid and glass with rubbing alcohol. The glass can then be siliconed in the place the screen was in.

Glass will be placed on the underside of the lid, replacing the screen's exact location. Using black colored silicone helps mask its use and disguise excess silicone. Any excess silicone that squeezes between the glass and lid can be smoothed out with a silicone tool or old gift card.

Step 3: Allow the silicone seal to dry and cure for 24 hours. Once dried, any excess silicone can be removed with a razor blade.

Glass Cutting 101

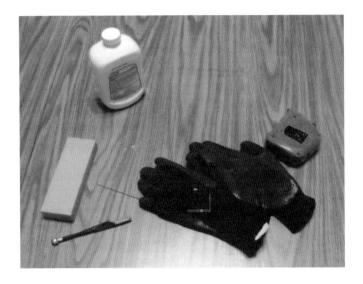

Glass cutting can be a simple task given the proper equipment and safety precaution. Be sure to wear gloves and eye protection when cutting glass. Cutting should be done in an area easy for clean up as there will be fine glass pieces from cutting and breaking the glass. Single strength glass and a glass cutter wheel can be purchased from a hardware store. Many stores provide custom cutting and this is an option for hobbyists not comfortable with cutting glass or who do not have a safe area for cutting.

 **Step 1:** Measure out the amount of glass needed to complete a lid. Use a permanent marker to make markings on the glass. Dip the glass cutter wheel into mineral oil. This is needed to keep the wheel lubricated. Using a straightedge, firmly press the glass cutting wheel against the glass starting at one of the edges and finish cutting through the opposite end. **<u>Only take one swipe through the glass with the cutter.</u>**

Step 2: Firmly grip the glass and break it from the line created with the glass cutter. This is the most difficult part. Many times the glass may shatter past the cut or the break many not be clean. Any unclean breaks can 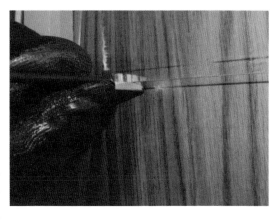 be removed with the glass breaker on the opposite side of the cutting wheel, or with pliers.

Step 3: Finish by filing down sharp edges using a file or polishing stone used for knife sharpening.

Vertical Aquarium Modifications

Arboreal species require a vertical aquarium that allows room for movement and breeding. Adapting a horizontal aquarium into a vertical terrarium can be very simple. Online hobbyist retailers often have conversion kits available for purchase. Whether using a premade kit or using cut glass, prep the aquarium by cleaning the outer and inner brim of the aquarium with rubbing alcohol.

Step 1: Arrange a standard aquarium vertically so the open "top" of the aquarium is now the "front." Custom cut three sheets of glass that combine together to create a lid that covers the entire opening of what is traditionally the "top" of the aquarium. When creating the three sections, imagine the aquarium broken into 6^{ths} with 3/6 as a bottom, 2/6 as a door, and 1/6 as a location for a latch. These divisions of glass do not have to be exact, but keep in mind the bottom must hold the drainage layer and substrate.

Step 2: To secure the lid in place, apply silicone inside the lip of the aquarium where the lip and glass meet. This area will not be tightly sealed without silicone. Failure to complete this step will lead to a leaking vertical tank. First, silicone the bottom and top pieces into place. The center piece of glass, which will serve as a door, can then be set into place.

Step 3: Next attach acrylic hardware, which can be purchased from glass shops or online terrarium retailers. Use silicone to attach a piano hinge to secure the center and bottom pieces of glass together. Attach the latch with silicone so the top and center pieces of glass will be secured together. Finally, apply silicone to the handle of the door to keep it in place. Let the silicone set and dry for 24 hours. Then allow the door to remain open for a few hours to allow the fumes to filter out before introducing frogs to the terrarium.

DIY: Ultrasonic Fogger

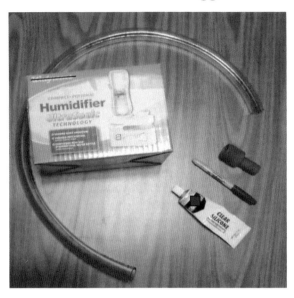

Ultrasonic foggers have become a popular habitat accessory. Given their price and limited size, a homemade version can be produced at a fraction of the cost and be created to use on large terrariums. These foggers should only be used a few minutes a day to increase humidity in a terrarium.

Step 1: Obtain a humidifier. Ultrasonic humidifiers can be purchased at a local pharmacy or retailer. Small, personal or travel humidifiers work for up to 29 gallon aquariums. Larger humidifiers can be used for larger terrariums.

Step 2: Remove the mist nozzle and replace it with a threaded to barbed connector. The barbed side is needed to connect to rubber tubing that transfers the fog from the humidifier into the tank. For a personal/travel humidifier a 1 inch thread to a ¾ inch barbed is required.

Step 3: Silicone the threaded side into the mist nozzle location. The best way to get a tight seal is to place silicone around the thread. Position the connector and allow it to set and dry for 24 hours.

Step 4: Place rubber hosing onto the connector and attach it to the tank. If the tank has a screen lid, then the outlet line can be placed on the screen. If this is not the case, a hole will need to be drilled into the glass or acrylic lid. Another 1 inch thread to a ¾ inch barbed connector will be needed. Attach the outlet line to the barbed side. A cap for the threaded end can be used to hold the line in place. Holes can be drilled into the cap to allow the fog to enter the tank, but not allow the frogs to escape. A larger hole can be drilled into the cap and insect proof fiberglass screen can be hot glued or silicone into the cap to prevent frogs from escaping.

Captive What?

Abbreviations and Terms Used When Listing on Classified Ads for Reptiles and Amphibians

Originally published in the *Herp Alert* the newsletter of Central Illinois Herpetological Society, portions have been updated and adapted.

There can be confusion concerning the meaning of specific terms used when producing, selling, and purchasing reptiles and amphibians in today's market. Abbreviations are often used within descriptions of animal classifieds. It is left to the integrity of the seller to state the animal's origin and sex within their advertisement. Below is a list of commonly used terms and their definitions.

1.0.0: Numbers in specific positions are used to identify the number and sex of animals being sold. The number in the first position designates the number of male animals in the seller's inventory. In this case there is one male for sale.

0.1.0: The number in the second position designates the number of female animals in the seller's inventory. In this case there is one female for sale.

0.0.1: The number in the third position designates the number of unsexed animals in the seller's inventory. These animals may be juveniles or just of undetermined sex. In this case there is one unsexed animal for sale.

Example: 2.4.3 indicates the seller has 2 males, 4 females, and 3 unsexed specimens in his inventory.

Wild Caught (WC): These are animals that are taken straight from the wild, plain and simple. Most of these animals do not survive. They are dehydrated, stressed, and many contain internal and external parasites. Quarantine is a must for these specimens.

Long Term Captive (LTC): This is a term that can be confusing and unclear. It refers to wild caught animals that have been in captivity for a period of time, as opposed to recently imported animals. What one person considers "long term" may differ from someone else. This term should be used lightly. Caution should be taken with these specimens in regards to parasites. The author notes that this term is best used for animals kept for several months to a year in captivity.

Captive Hatched (CH): These are reptiles that are produced from recently wild caught imports. Many females captured will be gravid, recently bred, or retaining sperm. They then give birth or lay eggs in the weeks or months after they have been brought into captivity. This is a very common term to see on price lists when species come in and lay eggs at an importer's facility. Sperm retention varies by species, but most wild caught animals that produce young in the first year after they are captured can be considered captive hatched. Most of these animals fair very well in captivity and can be a good bargain for purchasers. This term is not used for amphibians since they use external fertilization.

Captive Bred (CB): These are animals that are produced from a mated pair in captivity. For the most part, after a wild caught reptile has been in captivity for over a year, its offspring is considered to be captive bred. Amphibians can only produce captive bred offspring since they undergo external fertilization.

Farm Raised (FR): These are animals that are kept in outside environments, many in the country of their origin. There is a lot of speculation that these animals are taken straight from the wild and placed in these facilities to be sold. This can be true in many situations. However, companies such as Fluker's® Farms have created true farms for animals outside of their country of origin and sell the offspring to many chain pet stores. Fluker's® facility in El Salvador has produced "cherry headed" red footed tortoises, bearded dragons, and panther chameleons. As the reptile and amphibian market has become more mainstream in the pet trade, reptile and amphibian farms are starting in the United States in states such as Arizona, Texas, and Florida.

Conservation Projects: There are true frog farms in South America. Through the work of people like Sean Stewart and Mark Pepper there are farms producing frogs in their native habitat and legally importing them into the United States and Canada. These projects fund the purchasing of habitat and protect it. These projects have brought many new species into the hobby.

Remember best practice will protect a hobbyist's animals, collection, and investment. Quarantine all newly acquired wildlife whether it is wild caught, long term captive, captive hatched, captive bred, or farm raised, even if the animal is acquired through a reputable source.

References

Bowerman, J., Rombough, C., Weinstock, S., & Padgett-Flohr, G. (2010). Terbinafine Hydrochloride in Ethanol Effectively Clears Batrachochytrium dendrobatidis in Amphibians. *Journal of Herpetological Medicine and Surgery*, *20*(1), 24-28.

Captive Bred, Fluker Farms Price List. (2008, October 3). *Fluker Farms International*. Retrieved from: http://www.flukerfarms.com/PDFs/Captive-Bred.pdf

El Salvador- Reptile Ranch. (2008, October 3). *Fluker Farms*. Retrieved from: http://www.flukerfarms.com/tour/elsalvador/ranch.htm

Klingenberg, R. (2007). *Understanding Reptile Parasites* (2 ed.). Irvine, California: Advanced Vivarium Systems.

Kowalski, E. (n.d.). Euthanasia. *Caudata Culture Articles-Caudata.org*. Retrieved from: http://www.caudata.org/cc/articles/euthanasia.shtml

Longcore, J.E., A.P. Pessier and D.K. Nichols. (1999). Batrachochytrium dendrobatidis gen. et sp. nov., a chytrid pathogenic to amphibians. Mycologia 91:219-227.

Master, T. L. (1998): Dendrobates auratus (Black-and-green poison dart frog). Predation. Herp. Rev. 29: 164-165.

Moffett, M. W. (1995, May). Poison-Dart Frogs. *National Geographic*, *187*, 98-111.

Myers, C. W., Daly, J. W., & Malkin, B. (1978). A Dangerously Toxic New Frog (Phyllobates) Used By Embera Indians of Western Colombia, With Discussion of Blowgun Fabrication And Dart Poisoning. *Bulletin of the American Museum of Natural History*, *161*(2), 309-365.

Myers, C. W., & Daly, J. W. (1983, February). Dart-Poison Frogs. *Scientific American*, *248*(2), 120-133.

Oliver, James, and Charles Shaw. (1953).Amphibians and Reptiles of Hawaiian Islands. *Zoologica*. 38: 79.

Torreilles, S. L., McClure, D. E., & Green, S. L. (2009). Evaluation and Refinement of Euthanasia Methods for Xenopus Laevis. *Journal of the American Association for Laboratory Animal Science*, *48*(5), 512-516.

Wright, K. (2009). How I Treat Nematodes in Frogs. *Proceedings of the 2009 North American Veterinary Conference*, 1826.

Wright, K. (2009). How I Manage Wounds in Frogs. *Proceedings of the 2009 North American Veterinary Conference*, 1827.

Additional Information

Poisonfrogs.net: Conservation through Captive Breeding and Education. This is the author's site for dart frogs.

Association of Reptilian and Amphibian Veterinarians
Also known as the ARAV, this is the first organization to check for a local veterinarians practicing on reptiles and amphibians.
www.arav.org

Kingsnake.com: Several reptile and amphibian breeders/jobbers/businesses in the United States list their offspring/livestock here for sale.

Saurian.net: Patrick Nabors has supplied several well known zoos, aquaria, and institutions. His website is full of information and his availability of frogs.

Joshsfrogs.com: Josh has a wide variety of herpetological supplies. He is a great source for fruit flies and other feeder insects.

Black Jungle Terrarium Supply
Frogs, Plants, Supplies, and Feeders
Retail Location:
370 Avenue A
Turners Falls, MA. 01376
www.blackjungle.com

MistKing: Quality Misting Systems
1-877-MIST-123
www.mistking.com

Forums:

The great part about forums is the opportunity to ask fellow enthusiasts how they keep and propagate dart frogs. They are great places to post pictures of terrariums, get quick responses to questions, and find frogs for sale or trade. Here are a few forms:

Dartden.com   Dartfrogz.com   Dendroboard.com

Conservation Groups:

Treewalkers International
www.treewalkers.org

Amphibian Ark
www.amphibianark.org

Declining Amphibians Populations Task Force
www.canvamphibs.com

Dendrobates.org
www.dendrobates.org

USArk: United States Association of Reptiles Keepers
Protecting your rights to own reptiles and amphibians in captivity.
www.usark.org

Index

***Bold** print denotes photograph.

Checklists

Terrarium Building Supplies

- ✓ aquarium or terrarium
- ✓ custom cut lid out of glass or plexi/polycarbonate
- ✓ light
- ✓ egg crate, LECA, gravel (or combination)
- ✓ rocks/gravel (rinsed, optional)
- ✓ PVC pipe fittings
- ✓ window screen (not aluminum) or landscaping fabric
- ✓ orchid bark, milled sphagnum peat, coco fiber
- ✓ live plants, bromeliads, pothos, moss, ect.
- ✓ leaf litter (purchased or pesticide/herbicide free)
- ✓ coconut hut, or coconut for DIY
- ✓ hand sprayer
- ✓ silicone (optional)
- ✓ clay kitty litter (optional)
- ✓ door handles (optional)

Before Buying Frogs

- ✓ Understand the requirements needed for the proper care of dart frogs.
- ✓ Build and establish a terrarium.
- ✓ Establish food sources and culturing techniques.
- ✓ Determine what species fits the tank size and interests.
- ✓ Find a local breeder or reputable source of frogs.
- ✓ Ask questions and feel comfortable about the purchase.
- ✓ Purchase frogs and continue to gain knowledge on dart frog care and husbandry.

Made in the USA
Lexington, KY
04 January 2013